We ho
this journal and remember
your journey starts here

If you can spare a few moments, please leave us a review.
We are very interested in your feedback to create even better
products for you to enjoy in the near future.

Visit our website at amazing-notebooks.com or scan the QR code
below to see all of our awesome and creative products!

Thank you very much!

Amazing Notebooks

www.amazing-notebooks.com

Dear Bro,

I will always
love you and
miss you with
all my heart

...

Until we meet again.

I will love you forever Bro

Daily thoughts:

I will always love you and miss you with all my heart…

Daily thoughts:

I will always love you and miss you with all my heart...

Daily thoughts:

I will always love you and miss you with all my heart…

Daily thoughts:

I will always love you and miss you with all my heart...

Daily thoughts:

I will always love you and miss you with all my heart…

Daily thoughts:

I will always love you and miss you with all my heart...

Daily thoughts:

I will always love you and miss you with all my heart…

Daily thoughts:

I will always love you and miss you with all my heart...

Daily thoughts:

I will always love you and miss you with all my heart…

Daily thoughts:

I will always love you and miss you with all my heart...

Daily thoughts:

I will always love you and miss you with all my heart…

Daily thoughts:

I will always love you and miss you with all my heart…

Daily thoughts:

I will always love you and miss you with all my heart…

Daily thoughts:

I will always love you and miss you with all my heart…

Daily thoughts:

I will always love you and miss you with all my heart…

Daily thoughts:

I will always love you and miss you with all my heart…

Daily thoughts:

I will always love you and miss you with all my heart…

Daily thoughts:

I will always love you and miss you with all my heart…

Daily thoughts:

I will always love you and miss you with all my heart…

Daily thoughts:

I will always love you and miss you with all my heart…

Daily thoughts:

I will always love you and miss you with all my heart...

Daily thoughts:

I will always love you and miss you with all my heart...

Daily thoughts:

I will always love you and miss you with all my heart…

Daily thoughts:

I will always love you and miss you with all my heart…

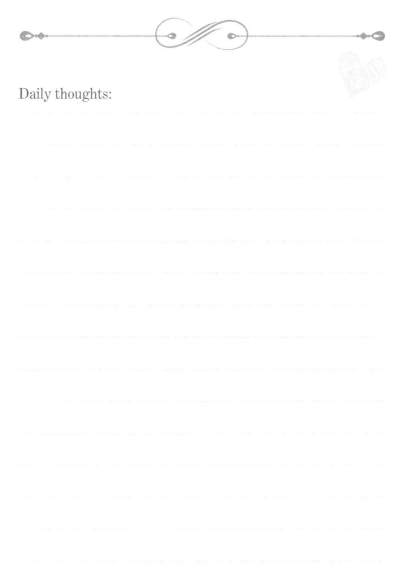

Daily thoughts:

I will always love you and miss you with all my heart…

Daily thoughts:

I will always love you and miss you with all my heart…

Daily thoughts:

I will always love you and miss you with all my heart…

Daily thoughts:

I will always love you and miss you with all my heart…

Daily thoughts:

I will always love you and miss you with all my heart…

Daily thoughts:

I will always love you and miss you with all my heart…

Daily thoughts:

I will always love you and miss you with all my heart…

Daily thoughts:

I will always love you and miss you with all my heart...

Daily thoughts:

I will always love you and miss you with all my heart…

Daily thoughts:

I will always love you and miss you with all my heart…

Daily thoughts:

I will always love you and miss you with all my heart…

Daily thoughts:

I will always love you and miss you with all my heart…

Daily thoughts:

I will always love you and miss you with all my heart...

Daily thoughts:

I will always love you and miss you with all my heart…

Daily thoughts:

I will always love you and miss you with all my heart…

Daily thoughts:

I will always love you and miss you with all my heart…

Daily thoughts:

I will always love you and miss you with all my heart...

Daily thoughts:

I will always love you and miss you with all my heart...

Daily thoughts:

I will always love you and miss you with all my heart…

Daily thoughts:

I will always love you and miss you with all my heart…

Daily thoughts:

_____

_____

_____

_____

_____

_____

_____

_____

_____

_____

_____

_____

_____

I will always love you and miss you with all my heart...

Daily thoughts:

I will always love you and miss you with all my heart…

Daily thoughts:

I will always love you and miss you with all my heart…

Daily thoughts:

I will always love you and miss you with all my heart…

Daily thoughts:

I will always love you and miss you with all my heart…

Daily thoughts:

I will always love you and miss you with all my heart…

Daily thoughts:

I will always love you and miss you with all my heart…

Daily thoughts:

I will always love you and miss you with all my heart…

Daily thoughts:

I will always love you and miss you with all my heart…

Daily thoughts:

I will always love you and miss you with all my heart…

Daily thoughts:

I will always love you and miss you with all my heart...

Daily thoughts:

I will always love you and miss you with all my heart…

Daily thoughts:

I will always love you and miss you with all my heart…

Daily thoughts:

I will always love you and miss you with all my heart...

Daily thoughts:

I will always love you and miss you with all my heart…

Daily thoughts:

I will always love you and miss you with all my heart…

Daily thoughts:

I will always love you and miss you with all my heart…

Daily thoughts:

I will always love you and miss you with all my heart…

Daily thoughts:

I will always love you and miss you with all my heart…

Daily thoughts:

I will always love you and miss you with all my heart…

Daily thoughts:

I will always love you and miss you with all my heart…

Daily thoughts:

I will always love you and miss you with all my heart…

Daily thoughts:

I will always love you and miss you with all my heart…

Daily thoughts:

I will always love you and miss you with all my heart…

Daily thoughts:

I will always love you and miss you with all my heart…

Daily thoughts:

I will always love you and miss you with all my heart…

Daily thoughts:

I will always love you and miss you with all my heart…

Daily thoughts:

I will always love you and miss you with all my heart…

Daily thoughts:

I will always love you and miss you with all my heart…

Daily thoughts:

I will always love you and miss you with all my heart…

Daily thoughts:

I will always love you and miss you with all my heart…

Daily thoughts:

I will always love you and miss you with all my heart…

Daily thoughts:

I will always love you and miss you with all my heart...

Daily thoughts:

I will always love you and miss you with all my heart…

Daily thoughts:

I will always love you and miss you with all my heart…

Daily thoughts:

I will always love you and miss you with all my heart…

Daily thoughts:

I will always love you and miss you with all my heart…

Daily thoughts:

I will always love you and miss you with all my heart…

Daily thoughts:

I will always love you and miss you with all my heart...

Daily thoughts:

I will always love you and miss you with all my heart…

Daily thoughts:

I will always love you and miss you with all my heart...

Daily thoughts:

I will always love you and miss you with all my heart…

Daily thoughts:

I will always love you and miss you with all my heart…

Daily thoughts:

I will always love you and miss you with all my heart…

Daily thoughts:

I will always love you and miss you with all my heart…

Daily thoughts:

I will always love you and miss you with all my heart…

Daily thoughts:

I will always love you and miss you with all my heart…

Daily thoughts:

I will always love you and miss you with all my heart...

Daily thoughts:

I will always love you and miss you with all my heart…

Daily thoughts:

I will always love you and miss you with all my heart…

Daily thoughts:

I will always love you and miss you with all my heart…

Daily thoughts:

I will always love you and miss you with all my heart…

Daily thoughts:

I will always love you and miss you with all my heart…

Daily thoughts:

I will always love you and miss you with all my heart…

Daily thoughts:

I will always love you and miss you with all my heart…

Daily thoughts:

I will always love you and miss you with all my heart...

Daily thoughts:

I will always love you and miss you with all my heart…

Daily thoughts:

I will always love you and miss you with all my heart…

Daily thoughts:

I will always love you and miss you with all my heart...

Daily thoughts:

I will always love you and miss you with all my heart…

Daily thoughts:

I will always love you and miss you with all my heart...

Daily thoughts:

I will always love you and miss you with all my heart...

Daily thoughts:

I will always love you and miss you with all my heart…

Daily thoughts:

I will always love you and miss you with all my heart…

Daily thoughts:

I will always love you and miss you with all my heart…

Daily thoughts:

I will always love you and miss you with all my heart…

Daily thoughts:

I will always love you and miss you with all my heart…

Daily thoughts:

I will always love you and miss you with all my heart...

Daily thoughts:

I will always love you and miss you with all my heart…

Daily thoughts:

I will always love you and miss you with all my heart…

Daily thoughts:

I will always love you and miss you with all my heart…

Daily thoughts:

I will always love you and miss you with all my heart…

Daily thoughts:

I will always love you and miss you with all my heart...

Daily thoughts:

I will always love you and miss you with all my heart…

Daily thoughts:

I will always love you and miss you with all my heart…

Daily thoughts:

I will always love you and miss you with all my heart…

Daily thoughts:

I will always love you and miss you with all my heart…

Daily thoughts:

I will always love you and miss you with all my heart…

Daily thoughts:

I will always love you and miss you with all my heart…

Daily thoughts:

I will always love you and miss you with all my heart…

Daily thoughts:

I will always love you and miss you with all my heart…

Daily thoughts:

I will always love you and miss you with all my heart…

Daily thoughts:

I will always love you and miss you with all my heart...

Daily thoughts:

I will always love you and miss you with all my heart…

Daily thoughts:

I will always love you and miss you with all my heart…

Daily thoughts:

I will always love you and miss you with all my heart…

Daily thoughts:

I will always love you and miss you with all my heart…

Daily thoughts:

I will always love you and miss you with all my heart…

Daily thoughts:

I will always love you and miss you with all my heart…

Daily thoughts:

I will always love you and miss you with all my heart…

Daily thoughts:

I will always love you and miss you with all my heart…

We hope you`ll enjoy this journal and remember your journey starts here

If you can spare a few moments, please leave us a review. We are very interested in your feedback to create even better products for you to enjoy in the near future.

Visit our website at amazing-notebooks.com or scan the QR code below to see all of our awesome and creative products!

Thank you very much!

Amazing Notebooks

www.amazing-notebooks.com

Made in the USA
Monee, IL
02 September 2021

77127760R00079